Calm Human Calm Horse

Essential Guide to Stay Calm During Rides & Emergencies, Cultivate Safety, Deepen Your Bond & Confidently Handle Stressful Situations

Bettyann Cernese

Breezy Knoll Innovations LLC

© **Copyright Bettyann Cernese 2024 - All rights reserved.**
Published by Breezy Knoll Innovations LLC

Under no circumstances will any blame or legal responsibility be held against the publisher, or author, for any damages, reparation, or monetary loss due to the information contained within this book. Either directly or indirectly. You are responsible for your own choices, actions, and results.

Legal Notice:
This book is copyright protected. This book is only for personal use. You cannot amend, distribute, sell, use, quote or paraphrase any part, of the content within this book, without the consent of the author or publisher.

Disclaimer Notice:
Please note the information contained within this document is for educational and entertainment purposes only. All effort has been expended to present accurate, up-to-date, and reliable, complete information. No warranties of any kind are declared or implied. Readers acknowledge that the author is not engaging in the rendering of legal, financial, medical or professional advice. The content within this book has been derived from various sources. Please consult a licensed professional before attempting any techniques outlined in this book.

By reading this document, the reader agrees that under no circumstances is the author responsible for any losses, direct or indirect, which are incurred as a result of the use of the information contained within this document, including, but not limited to, — errors, omissions, or inaccuracies.

Book Cover Photo by Lou Genovese, www.one27photo.com

Contents

1. Introduction   1
2. Living in the Moment   7
   How Horses Perceive and Respond to Their World
   How Horses Categorize Experiences
   Motivations of Horse Behavior
   Guided Practice
3. The Human Influence   17
   Silent Signals
   The Importance of Presence
   Guided Practice: Presence
   The Emotional Mirror
   Science of Emotions
   Guided Practice: The Quick Coherence® Technique
   Examples of Emotional Influence
   Actionable Ways to Regulate Your Emotions

4. Inner Calm, Outer Connection 35
   - The Power of Self-Awareness
   - Mindfulness in Action: Techniques for Greater Self-Awareness
   - Decoding Your Emotions
   - Mastering Emotions
   - Guided Practice for Emotional Regulation and Calmness

5. Make a Difference with Your Review 43
   - Unlock the Power of Generosity

6. Confident in Crisis 47
   - Preparing for and Managing Stressful Situations
   - Lay the Groundwork to Enhance Trust and Readiness for Emergencies
   - Staying Calm During Emergencies

7. Ready for Anything 57
   - Assessing and Handling Equine Emergencies
   - Practical Steps to Ensure Preparedness
   - Healing Together
   - Post-Emergency Recovery for Horse and Handler
   - Reinforcing Readiness for the Future

8. Conclusion	69
Pay It Forward!	
References	73
About the author	75

Chapter 1
Introduction

"Horses teach you a lot. Very little of it actually has to do with horses."
　　　　　　　　　　Anthony T. Hincks

HAVE YOU EVER EXPERIENCED a moment where your horse was afraid? Perhaps you've seen your horse alert and freeze, eyes wide with the whites showing, nostrils flaring, ears pointed forward, head held high, and muscles tense. In that instant, did you notice what happened within yourself? Did you tense up, freeze, or feel a surge of worry or fear? While your ears may not have pointed forward, your eyes likely widened, your nostrils flared, and your muscles tightened. In such moments, one of you needs to pivot, to shift that energy, and that someone is you. As prey animals, horses' survival instincts prompt them to pivot and run.

Whether you are a horse owner or rider, no matter your experience level, an equestrian trainer or instructor, an equine therapist or veterinarian, you've likely encountered the fear/flight response of a horse. Horses react to perceived danger by running to survive and respond in whatever way they can to ensure their safety.

I decided to write this book because, in my 30 years of working with horses, I've learned that they are incredibly attuned to our feelings and emotions, responding accordingly. By learning to regulate our emotions, we can help them adjust theirs, making all the difference in stressful situations or emergencies for both human and horse.

If you search for "What is the first rule in any emergency," you'll find advice like assessing the situation, checking the scene for safety, or looking for danger. I know this firsthand from my 35 years with the National Ski Patrol, helping injured skiers—safety first for humans, then assessing the situation.

With horses, an emergency often arises when they are in a heightened state or about to enter one due to something they perceive as a threat. This might be a "scary" plastic bag blowing in the wind, an unexpected dog or other animal encounter on a trail ride, or an injury requiring emergency medical care.

From my experiences working with humans and horses, I've learned that the most crucial step is to remain calm. You must remain calm to think clearly and assess the situation, which is often the hardest thing to do, especially with horses. As prey animals, their first instinct is flight, and that heightened response is palpable.

In this book, I will share practical techniques to help both you and your horse remain calm in stressful situations or emergencies. These simple yet effective practices will create a safer environment, strengthen your bond, and enable you to handle challenging situations confidently.

This book serves as your essential guide to maintaining calmness during rides and emergencies. It will enhance your ability to stay composed in any circumstance. You'll improve your communication with your horse, increase confidence in managing emergencies and everyday challenges, and learn practical techniques to achieve these outcomes.

In the following chapters, you will explore the world through your horse's eyes, understanding how they perceive and respond to their environment. You'll learn about the profound influence you have on your horse's behavior through your presence and emotions. We'll delve into self-awareness and emotional regulation techniques, which are crucial for staying calm and building trust. Finally, you'll discover how to prepare for and handle stressful situations confidently, ensuring you and your horse can face any challenge together.

Before we begin, I encourage you to grab a notebook and pen to journal your experiences as you work through this book. Writing down your thoughts, observations, and reflections can be incredibly beneficial. Journaling helps you process your emotions, track your progress, and deepen your understanding of the techniques you'll be learning. Putting pen to paper engages different brain parts, enhancing memory retention and clarity. This practice will help you internalize the lessons and document your journey with your horse, creating a valuable resource you can refer back to and learn from over time.

Join me on this journey to becoming a calm human for a calm horse. We will create a harmonious partnership based on trust, understanding, and mutual respect.

> ### **Want to Take Your Journey Even Further?**
>
> By implementing what you learn in this book, you will make great strides toward a calm, trust-filled connection with your horse! Now, let's go even deeper. Your path to a more profound emotional and energetic connection with your horse has just begun—click the link or scan the code to continue your journey!
> **Visit tab.so/calmhorse**
>
>

Chapter 2
Living in the Moment

"To understand a horse is to be loved by a horse."

Tom Dorrance

How Horses Perceive and Respond to Their World

IMAGINE STANDING NEXT TO your horse in a quiet field. The gentle breeze rustles the leaves, and you notice your horse's ears twitching towards a distant sound that you can barely hear. Horses are among the most perceptive creatures, with their senses finely tuned to detect even the slightest changes in their environment. This heightened perception is a crucial survival tool, allowing them to respond swiftly to potential threats. As prey animals, their acute senses of sight, sound, and smell are their first lines of defense. Understanding this helps us appreciate the delicate balance of their world and the depth of their sensory experience.

How Horses Categorize Experiences

Horses have a unique way of categorizing their experiences and shaping their behavior and reactions. They often categorize stimuli into safe or unsafe, familiar or unfamiliar. These categories are formed through repeated experiences and the outcomes of those experiences. Positive experiences reinforce a sense of safety and familiarity, while negative experiences can lead to caution or fear. For instance, a horse that encounters a noisy tractor for the first time might react with alarm, but with repeated calm and positive exposures, the tractor becomes a familiar, non-threatening part of their environment. By understanding this process, we can better guide our horses through new experiences, helping them form positive associations.

Motivations of Horse Behavior

At the heart of horse behavior lies a simple yet powerful motivation: the pursuit of safety and comfort. These motivations drive almost every action a horse takes. In the wild, a horse's survival depends on staying alert to danger and finding safe grazing grounds. Domesticated horses retain these instincts, constantly seeking to feel secure and at ease. When a horse feels threatened, its primary response is to flee. Conversely, when a horse feels safe and comfortable, it exhibits relaxed behaviors such as grazing, resting, and socializing. Recognizing these motivations helps us create environments and interactions that fulfill our horses' innate needs.

Horses want safety and comfort

Safety and comfort are paramount to a horse's well-being. A horse that feels safe is more likely to be calm, responsive, and willing to engage. Conversely, a horse that feels threatened or uncomfortable may exhibit behaviors such as bolting, rearing, or refusing to follow commands. Our role as caretakers is to provide an environment where our horses feel secure and comfortable. This involves consistent routines, gentle handling, and positive reinforcement. By doing so, we not only enhance their physical well-being but also their emotional and psychological health.

Horses live in the present moment

Horses are remarkable in their ability to live fully in the present moment, a trait that is deeply ingrained in their survival instincts. Unlike humans, who often get caught up in thoughts about the past or future, horses are acutely aware of their immediate surroundings, fully engaging their senses to monitor their environment for any signs of danger.

Their keen senses facilitate horses' heightened state of awareness. Their eyes are positioned on the sides of their heads, providing a wide field of vision covering nearly 350 degrees. This panoramic vision allows them to detect movement from almost any direction, a crucial adaptation for spotting predators. Horses also have excellent night vision, enabling them to navigate and remain vigilant even in low-light conditions.

Their sense of hearing is equally impressive. Horses can rotate their ears almost 180 degrees to capture sounds from various directions. This ability to pinpoint the source of a sound helps them stay alert to potential threats. They can detect frequencies ranging from low to high, including sounds that are beyond the range of human hearing.

The sense of smell plays a vital role in how horses perceive their world. With large, sensitive nostrils, horses can detect subtle scents the wind carries, allowing them to identify other animals, food, and potential dangers long before they are visible.

Living in the present moment also means that horses are highly responsive to their immediate physical sensations. They are sensitive to changes in temperature, the feel of the ground beneath their hooves, and the touch of their rider or handler. This acute sensitivity makes them excellent at reading humans' body language and emotional state. A horse can sense if a person is tense, nervous, or calm, often mirroring these emotions.

Adopting a mindset similar to horses by being fully present can significantly improve our interactions with them. *Focusing on the here and now makes us more attuned to our horse's subtle cues and behaviors.* This heightened awareness helps build a deeper bond based on trust and mutual understanding. As we strive to be present, we create a calm and supportive environment where both horse and human can thrive.

By appreciating how horses engage all their senses to stay grounded in the present moment, we can learn to better support their needs and enhance our relationship with them.

Guided Practice

Part 1 - Observe Your Horse

Before you begin, grab your notebook or journal and a pen.

To deepen your understanding of your horse's behavior, try this simple yet powerful exercise: Spend some quiet time observing your horse. Notice how they respond to different stimuli in their environment. Pay attention to their body language, ear movements, eyes, nostrils, and vocalizations. What do they do when they feel relaxed? By observing your horse without interference, you'll gain valuable insights into their perception of the world and their unique way of processing experiences.

Part 2 - Observe What Your Horse Observes

The next step in this practice is to shift your attention to what it is that your horse is observing.

- As they look at something, look as well. What do you see?

- What might they be observing? Look around; what else do you see?

- What do you hear?

- Turn your head towards the sound. Is there something you notice or see as you follow the sound?

- Shift your attention to your skin, what do you feel? Maybe the sleeve of your shirt on your arm, or the movement of the air across your face.

- Notice if there is any odor or scent in the air; what do you smell?

- As you observe your senses, what you are feeling, does any emotion arise, such as concern or worry, and if so, how quickly does it return to neutral, calm, or content?

Welcome to the world of your horse! They are constantly in tune with all of their senses, and as you learn to pay more attention to observing what your horse observes, you will be more informed about their behavior and actions.

> *This practice enhances your bond and equips you with the knowledge to better support your horse's needs.*

In this chapter, we've explored the perceptive nature of horses and how they categorize their experiences, driven by the fundamental needs for safety and comfort. By appreciating their motivations and ability to live in the present moment, we can improve our interactions and create a more harmonious relationship. As we move forward, we'll delve into the profound impact humans have on horse behavior, highlighting the importance of presence and emotional connection in shaping a calm and trusting partnership.

Chapter 3
The Human Influence

Shaping Horse Behavior through Presence and Emotion

> *He knows when you're happy. He knows when you're comfortable. He knows when you're confident. And he always knows when you have treats.*
>
> Anonymous

Silent Signals

Body language is a fundamental aspect of communication with horses. Horses are non-verbal creatures, relying heavily on visual and tactile cues to understand and interact with their environment. As a result, they are exceptionally adept at reading the body language of humans and other animals. For those who work with horses, mastering the art of body language can significantly enhance the relationship and effectiveness of interactions.

Effective Body Language

Consider the example of leading a horse. When you lead a horse with a confident, upright posture, your movements steady and deliberate, the horse is more likely to follow you calmly and obediently. Your body language conveys assurance and direction, helping the horse understand what is expected of them. Conversely, the horse may become confused or anxious if you approach the horse with slouched shoulders, shuffling feet, and hesitant movements. They pick up on the uncertainty in your posture and may mirror this nervous energy, leading to a less controlled and cooperative experience.

Another example is when mounting a horse. Before you even attempt to get on, your horse watches your every move. If you approach the horse with calm, deliberate movements and speak in a soft, soothing tone, the horse is likely to remain relaxed. However, if you are jittery, making sudden movements or loud noises, the horse can become skittish, sensing your anxiety. This can make the mounting process more challenging and potentially unsafe.

In the round pen, body language becomes even more crucial. Trainers often use their posture, gestures, and eye contact to communicate with the horse. For instance, to ask a horse to move forward, a trainer might step towards the horse with an assertive stance, directing their energy towards its hindquarters. To slow down or stop, the trainer might relax their posture, soften their gaze, and take a step back. These subtle cues can guide the horse's movements without needing physical contact.

Additionally, consider the act of grooming. Grooming is not just a practical activity but also a form of bonding. As you groom your horse, your body language should be relaxed and rhythmic. Horses enjoy the steady, predictable brushing movements, which can be soothing and reassuring. If you groom with hurried or erratic motions, the horse may become tense or unsettled, missing out on the calming benefits of the interaction.

Understanding the importance of body language also extends to recognizing your horse's signals. Horses use their body language to communicate their feelings and intentions. For example, a horse with relaxed ears, a lowered head, and a soft eye are likely to feel calm and content. In contrast, pinned ears, a high head, and wide eyes indicate fear or agitation. By learning to read these signs, you can adjust your body language to respond appropriately, creating a harmonious interaction.

Effective body language is more than just your actions; it's also about the energy you project. Horses are highly sensitive to the energy and intent behind your movements. Approaching with positive, calm energy fosters a sense of safety and trust. Your horse will respond more favorably when they sense that you are centered and confident.

Body language is a powerful tool in horse-human communication. You can significantly improve your interactions with horses by cultivating awareness of your posture, movements, and energy. Consistent, clear, and calm body language helps establish trust and clarity, making your horse more responsive and cooperative. Remember, your horse is always watching and interpreting your signals, so strive to be as clear and intentional with your body language as you are with your words.

The Importance of Presence

"Life is available only in the present moment."
                                             Thich Nhat Hanh

Being present with your horse is crucial for fostering a trusting relationship and effective communication. Horses live in the moment, fully engaged with their surroundings. When you are distracted, thinking about the past or future, or simply not fully present, it affects your horse's behavior and your ability to connect with them.

Imagine you are grooming your horse, but your mind is occupied with thoughts of a stressful meeting you had earlier in the day. Your strokes become inconsistent, and your energy is scattered.

Your horse senses this distraction and may become fidgety or uneasy, picking up on your unsettled energy. *Horses are incredibly perceptive and can sense when your attention is divided, leading to a lack of clear communication and potentially increasing their stress or anxiety.*

Another example is during a training session. If you are preoccupied with planning tomorrow's activities or replaying an argument from last night, your horse will notice. They may become confused by your inconsistent cues or lack of focus. This can lead to frustration for both you and your horse, hindering progress and damaging the bond you are trying to build.

> *"When we engage in the world without deliberate presence, we are reacting to the moment from a past perspective or an imagined future."*
> – Kelly Wendorf Flying Lead Change

Guided Practice: Presence

To be fully present with your horse, it is essential to develop mindfulness and focus. Here are some techniques to help you become more present when you are with your horse. As you practice each, what do you notice in yourself, and what do you notice about your horse? Consider journaling about your practices to uncover possible patterns for both you and your horse.

1. **Eliminate Distractions**: Put away your phone, clear your mind of other tasks, and dedicate this time solely to your horse. Treat these moments as sacred, deserving your full attention.

2. **Set Intentions**: Before starting any activity with your horse, set a clear intention for what you want to achieve. This could be simple, like "I want to create a calm and positive environment." Keeping this intention in mind helps maintain your focus.

3. **Deep Breathing**: Take a few deep breaths before interacting with your horse. Focus on the sensation of the breath entering and leaving your body, which helps center your mind and body. Here is a beautiful quote by Thich Nhat Hanh that you can say as you breathe to help shift from all other thoughts to bring yourself into the present moment: *"Breathing in, I calm body and mind. Breathing out, I smile. Dwelling in the present moment I know this is the only moment."*

4. **Ground Yourself**: Stand still and feel the ground beneath your feet. Visualize roots growing from your feet into the earth, anchoring you in the present moment. This can help you feel more stable and connected.

5. **Body Scan**: Mentally scan your body from head to toe, noticing any areas of tension. Consciously relax these areas, releasing any stress or distractions. **Tip:** As you notice an area of tension, imagine your breath moving into that area, and as you exhale, imagine the tension leaving with

your breath.

6. **Observe Your Horse**: Spend a few minutes simply watching your horse. Notice their body language, movements, and expressions. This will help you become more attuned to your horse and bring your focus to the present. Refer back to the guided practice in Chapter 2.

7. **Mindful Grooming**: Approach grooming as a meditative practice. Pay attention to the texture of your horse's coat, the rhythm of your strokes, and your horse's response. This can be a calming experience for both you and your horse.

By incorporating these techniques, you can cultivate a mindful presence that your horse will respond to positively.

> *When you are fully present, your horse feels safer, more understood, and more willing to engage. This creates a harmonious and trusting relationship where both you and your horse can thrive.*

Remember, your horse depends on you to be their anchor in the present moment. Practicing mindfulness and being fully present enhances your ability to communicate effectively, build trust, and create a more enjoyable and productive partnership with your horse.

The Emotional Mirror

> *"The horse is a mirror to your soul, and sometimes you might not like what you see in the mirror."*
>
> Buck Brannaman

Horses are highly sensitive animals, deeply attuned to the emotional states of those around them. When humans interact with horses, their emotions, whether positive or negative, are keenly perceived by these perceptive creatures. Understanding how human emotions affect horses is crucial for building a trusting and harmonious relationship.

Your Feelings Influence Your Horse

Horses respond to the emotions we project. For instance, if you approach your horse feeling anxious or stressed, your horse is likely to mirror those emotions. They may become restless, agitated, or even fearful. On the other hand, if you are calm, confident, and positive, your horse will feel more secure and relaxed.

This sensitivity is rooted in the horse's survival instincts as a prey animal. In the wild, a horse's ability to detect the emotions and intentions of other animals (including humans) can mean the difference between life and death. Consequently, horses have evolved to be exceptionally perceptive to the emotional cues of those around them.

Emotional Congruence Matters

Being congruent with our emotions—aligning what we feel inside with what we express outside—is vital when working with horses. Incongruence, such as smiling while feeling frustrated, can confuse a horse, leading to mistrust. Horses rely on clear and consistent signals from their handlers. When there is a mismatch between your internal state and your external expressions, it can create anxiety and confusion for the horse.

Science of Emotions

Heart coherence is a state where the heart, mind, and emotions align and work together harmoniously. This state is reflected in the heart's electromagnetic field, which is an energy field emitted by the heart that can be detected several feet away from the human body and as much as 25 feet away from a horse. Emotions such as love, gratitude, and appreciation generate a coherent heart pattern, while emotions like anger, frustration, and anxiety create an incoherent pattern.

Horses are highly sensitive to this electromagnetic field. Studies have shown that horses can detect and respond to humans' heart rhythms, often mirroring their handlers' emotional state. When you are in a state of heart coherence, your horse is more likely to feel calm and connected. Conversely, an incoherent heart pattern can lead to a stressed and unresponsive horse.

Guided Practice: The Quick Coherence® Technique

The Quick Coherence® Technique from The Institute of HeartMath® is a simple yet powerful practice that helps you achieve heart coherence. This technique can be highly beneficial when practiced before interacting with your horse and even while in your horse's presence. Here's how you can do it:

Step 1: Heart-Focused Breathing

- Focus your attention in the area of your heart. Imagine your breath is flowing in and out of your heart or chest area, breathing a little slower and deeper than usual.

- Inhale for 5 seconds, exhale for 5 seconds (or whatever rhythm is comfortable). Putting your attention around the heart area helps you center and get coherent. You can simply ask to be brought into heart-brain coherence. Also, it helps to maintain focus on your heart by placing your hand on it. You can also use the prayer mudra, palms together, and touch your heart.

Step 2: Activate a Positive or Renewing Feeling

- Make a sincere attempt to experience a regenerative feeling such as appreciation, care, love, and compassion for your horse or someone, something, or some place in your life.

- Try to re-experience the feeling you have for someone you love, a pet, a special place, an accomplishment, etc., or focus on a feeling of calm or ease. Feel this regenerative feeling deeply and do your best to sustain it. If your mind wanders, simply shift your focus to someone else and send love and compassion.

Practice Before Interacting with Your Horse: Engaging in the Quick Coherence® Technique before interacting with your horse helps you approach the interaction with a calm, centered, and coherent state of mind. Horses are highly sensitive to the emotional states of humans and can mirror your calmness and coherence, making them more relaxed and responsive.

Benefits of Practicing in the Presence of Your Horse: Practicing this technique while with your horse can further enhance your bond and communication. As you achieve heart coherence, your horse can sense the stable and positive energy you emit, which can help them feel more secure and connected to you. This practice not only aids in managing your own stress but also fosters a more harmonious and trusting relationship with your horse.

Examples of Emotional Influence

Consider a situation where you are leading your horse through a new and potentially scary environment. If you are nervous, your horse will likely pick up on your anxiety and become skittish. However, if you remain calm and confident, your horse will feel reassured and more willing to follow your lead.

Another example is during training sessions. A patient and positive trainer will foster a cooperative and willing horse. In contrast, a trainer who is frustrated or angry may create a resistant and fearful horse, as the horse senses and mirrors the negative emotions.

Actionable Ways to Regulate Your Emotions

1. **Use the Quick Coherence Technique®** outlined above.

2. **Practice Deep Breathing**: Deep, slow breathing can help calm your nervous system and create a sense of relaxation. Before interacting with your horse, take a few minutes to breathe deeply and center yourself.

3. **Engage in Mindfulness**: Mindfulness practices like meditation or yoga can help you stay present and manage your emotions effectively. Regular practice can enhance your ability to remain calm and focused around your horse.

4. **Use Positive Visualization**: Visualize positive outcomes and peaceful interactions with your horse. This can help shift your emotional state and create a

more positive energy that your horse will respond to.

5. **Develop Emotional Awareness**: Pay attention to your emotions and how they affect your body. By becoming more aware of your emotional triggers, you can take steps to manage them before they impact your horse.

6. **Cultivate Gratitude**: Practicing gratitude can shift your emotional state from negative to positive. Spend a few moments each day reflecting on what you are grateful for, which can enhance your overall emotional well-being.

By understanding the profound connection between human emotions and horse behavior, you can create a more harmonious and effective partnership with your horse. Practicing emotional congruence and achieving heart coherence can significantly improve your horse's responsiveness and trust.

·♥·♥·♥·♥·♥·

You're making great strides shaping your horse's behavior!

Now, let's go even deeper. Your path to a more profound emotional and energetic connection with your horse has just begun—*Visit tab.so/calmhorse or scan the code to continue your journey!*

·♥·♥·♥·♥·♥·

Chapter 4
Inner Calm, Outer Connection

Your horse doesn't respond to what you want, it responds to who you are being.
                                       Angie Wells

The Power of Self-Awareness

SELF-AWARENESS IS THE FOUNDATION of emotional mastery and is crucial when working with horses. It involves being conscious of your thoughts, emotions, and physical sensations in the present moment. When you are self-aware, you can recognize your emotional state and its impact on your interactions with your horse.

This awareness helps you stay grounded and present, essential for effective communication and building trust with your horse.

For example, if you notice that you are feeling anxious before a riding session, your self-awareness allows you to take steps to calm yourself before approaching your horse. This proactive approach prevents your anxiety from affecting your horse, allowing for a more positive and productive interaction.

Mindfulness in Action: Techniques for Greater Self-Awareness

Mindfulness is a powerful tool for developing self-awareness. It involves paying attention to the present moment without judgment. Here is a simple mindfulness technique to enhance self-awareness.

1. **Find a Quiet Space**: Choose a calm and quiet environment where you can sit comfortably without distractions.

2. **Focus on Your Breath**: Close your eyes and take slow, deep breaths. Pay attention to the sensation of the breath entering and

leaving your body.

3. **Scan Your Body**: Starting from the top of your head, mentally scan your body for any areas of tension or discomfort. Notice these sensations without trying to change them.

4. **Acknowledge Your Thoughts**: Observe your thoughts as they arise. Acknowledge them without judgment and gently bring your focus back to your breath.

5. **Stay Present**: Continue this practice for 5-10 minutes, staying present with your breath and body sensations.

Regular mindfulness practice helps you become more attuned to your emotional and physical states, enhancing your self-awareness and presence with your horse. Grab your journal & pen to capture your experience. You can also try this practice in the barn outside your horse's stall or sitting in a chair near their pasture.

Decoding Your Emotions

"Feelings are something you have; not something you are."

Shannon L. Alder

Recognizing Patterns to Improve Interactions

Everyone has emotional patterns—habitual ways of reacting to certain situations. These patterns can significantly impact your relationship with your horse. Understanding your emotional patterns involves recognizing the triggers that cause emotional reactions and observing how these reactions manifest in your body and behavior.

For instance, you might notice that you become frustrated when your horse doesn't respond as expected during training. By understanding this pattern, you can identify the trigger (e.g., your horse not following a cue) and the resulting emotion (frustration). This understanding allows you to take a step back and address the root cause of the frustration rather than reacting impulsively. I encourage you to get curious about your go-to emotions not only with your horse but also in your day-to-day life.

Mastering Emotions

The Art of Regulation for Greater Harmony

Emotional regulation is the ability to manage and respond to your emotions in a healthy and constructive manner. It involves recognizing your feelings, understanding their impact, and using strategies to influence them positively. Effective emotional regulation helps you maintain a calm and composed demeanor, which is vital when working with horses.

For example, if you feel anger rising during a training session, emotional regulation techniques can help you diffuse the anger and replace it with patience and understanding. This not only benefits you but also creates a safer and more trusting environment for your horse.

Guided Practice for Emotional Regulation and Calmness

Staying calm in challenging situations is essential for effective horse handling. Here is a technique to help regulate your emotions and maintain calmness:

1. **Breathe Deep**: Take 5 deep, diaphragmatic breaths to calm your nervous system. Inhale deeply through your nose, allowing your abdomen to expand, then exhale slowly through your mouth.

2. **Positive Visualization**: Visualize a calm and successful interaction with your horse. Imagine yourself responding to challenges with patience and confidence.

3. **Ground Yourself**: Stand with your feet firmly planted on the ground. Visualize roots growing from your feet into the earth, anchoring you in the present moment. This helps you feel stable and connected.

4. **Affirmations**: Use positive affirmations to reinforce a calm mindset. Repeat phrases like "I am calm and in control" or "My horse and I are connected and safe."

By practicing these techniques, you can effectively regulate your emotions, creating a calm and positive environment for your horse. If you feel overwhelmed, take a short break to regroup. Step away from the situation, take a few deep breaths, and return when you feel more composed. This is a perfect time to use the Quick Coherence® Technique outlined in Chapter 3.

Keep up the great work, you're making great strides toward a calm, trust-filled connection with your horse!

Now, let's go even deeper. Your path to a more profound emotional and energetic connection with your horse has just begun—*Visit tab.so/calmhorse or scan the code to continue your journey!*

Chapter 5
Make a Difference with Your Review

"Horses give us the wings we lack."
Pam Brown

Unlock the Power of Generosity

Helping others can bring joy to our lives. If we can share that joy through this book, why not try?

To make that happen, I have a question for you...

Would you help someone you've never met, even if you never got credit for it?

Who is this person you ask? They are just like you. Maybe less experienced with horses, wanting to make a difference, and needing help, but not sure where to look.

My mission is to make calm, confident horsemanship accessible to everyone. Everything I do stems from that mission. And, the only way to accomplish that mission is by reaching...well...everyone.

This is where you come in. Most people do, in fact, judge a book by its cover (and its reviews). **So here's my ask on behalf of a struggling horse lover you've never met:**

Please help that horse lover by leaving this book a review.

Your gift costs no money and less than 60 seconds to make real, but can change a fellow horse lover's life forever. **Your review could help...**

- *...one more horse owner build a stronger bond with their horse.*

- *...one more rider handle stressful situations with confidence.*

MAKE A DIFFERENCE WITH YOUR REVIEW

- *...one more trainer create a safe and calm environment.*

- *...one more veterinarian support their equine patients effectively.*

- *...one more dream of a harmonious horse-human relationship come true.*

To get that 'feel good' feeling and help this person for real, all you have to do is...and it takes less than 60 seconds... leave a review.

Simply scan the QR code below or go to https://tab.so/reviewchch to leave your review on Amazon.

If you feel good about helping a faceless horse lover, you are my kind of person! Welcome to the club. You're one of us.

I'm that much more excited to help you achieve calm and confidence with your horse faster and easier than you can possibly imagine. You'll love the lessons I'm about to share in the coming chapters.

Thank you from the bottom of my heart.

With heartfelt gratitude,
Bettyann Cernese

·♥·♥·♥·♥·♥·

PS - Fun fact: If you provide something of value to another person, it makes you more valuable to them. If you'd like goodwill straight from another horse lover - and you believe this book will help them - send this book their way.

Chapter 6
Confident in Crisis

"Luck is what happens when preparation meets opportunity."

Seneca

Preparing for and Managing Stressful Situations

Handling stressful situations with confidence is a crucial skill for any horse handler. This chapter will guide you in preparing both yourself and your horse for stressful situations, teaching you how to respond in the moment, and emphasizing the importance of practicing techniques in a relaxed environment to ensure you can calmly and confidently handle emergencies.

Lay the Groundwork to Enhance Trust and Readiness for Emergencies

Preparation is key to effectively managing stressful situations with your horse. By anticipating potential stressors and preparing in advance, you can significantly reduce the impact of these events on both you and your horse. This involves familiarizing your horse with various stimuli, practicing emergency procedures, and conditioning yourself to remain calm under pressure.

> *Incorporating the techniques explained in the previous chapters as part of your preparation will not only enhance your ability to handle emergencies but also deepen your bond, connection, and trust with your horse, leading to more positive outcomes.*

Familiarize Your Horse with Various Stimuli

One of the most effective ways to prepare for potential stressors is to expose your horse to different environments, sounds, and scenarios in a controlled setting. This desensitization process helps your horse become accustomed to various stimuli, reducing their likelihood of becoming overwhelmed in new or unexpected situations.

For example, you can introduce your horse to common outdoor noises such as a plastic bag rustling, bicycles, or barking dogs. Start by exposing them to these stimuli from a distance, gradually decreasing the distance as your horse becomes more comfortable. Throughout this process, use the techniques discussed in Chapters 4 mastering your emotions and staying calm & grounded. This will help your horse associate these potentially frightening stimuli with a sense of safety and calmness, provided by your consistent and composed demeanor.

Practice Emergency Procedures

Rehearsing emergency drills, such as quickly saddling or unsaddling your horse, can build muscle memory and confidence in your ability to manage actual emergencies. These practice sessions should be conducted in a calm and relaxed environment, allowing both you and your horse to learn and adapt without the pressure of an actual emergency.

Practice taking vital signs as well as touching your horse all over their body. Can you check his gums by lifting his lip? Can you touch all around his face and nostrils, around the genitals, inside the hind legs? These are all important things to practice so that if you do have an injury or emergency that requires treatment, your horse will be familiar with being touched in these places.

During these drills, focus on maintaining the emotional regulation and self-awareness techniques covered in Chapter 4. By practicing these techniques regularly, you train yourself to stay calm and focused, even when faced with high-pressure situations. This preparation not only improves your readiness but also reinforces the bond with your horse, as they learn to trust your steady and composed presence.

The Importance of Practicing Techniques

Incorporating the techniques from previous chapters into your routine is essential for effective preparation. These practices not only equip you with the tools needed to handle emergencies but also strengthen your relationship with your horse, creating a foundation of trust and mutual understanding.

For instance, mindfulness exercises and emotional regulation techniques can be integrated into your daily interactions with your horse. Spend a few minutes before each session to center yourself, using deep breathing and visualization to achieve a state of calm. Use the Quick Coherence Technique® to send love, care and appreciation to your horse. Approach your horse with this calm energy, and observe how they respond. Over time, your horse will become more attuned to your emotional state and more responsive to your calming influence.

Bond, Trust and Connection

Preparation is not just about readiness; it's about building a deeper connection with your horse. By consistently practicing these techniques, you demonstrate to your horse that you are a reliable and calm leader. This trust is crucial in stressful situations, as your horse will look to you for guidance and reassurance.

For example, if your horse encounters a startling situation, such as a sudden loud noise, your practiced calmness and steady presence can help them quickly recover and feel safe. This mutual trust and understanding create a positive feedback loop, where each successful handling of a stressful situation further strengthens your bond and improves your horse's confidence in you.

By preparing for stress before it arises, you create a safer and more predictable environment for both you and your horse. Familiarizing your horse with various stimuli, practicing emergency procedures, and consistently applying the techniques from previous chapters not only enhance your readiness but also deepen the bond and trust between you and your horse. This preparation ensures that, when faced with an actual emergency, you can respond calmly and effectively, leading to a more positive outcome for both you and your horse.

Staying Calm During Emergencies

Maintaining calm during an emergency is crucial. Your horse looks to you for cues on how to react, and your calm demeanor can significantly influence their behavior. To stay calm, focus on controlling your breath, maintaining a steady tone of voice, and using deliberate, slow movements.

For example, if your horse becomes startled by a loud noise, or your horse is severely injured and needs your immediate attention, taking deep, slow breaths and speaking to them in a soothing voice can help reassure them. Avoid sudden or erratic movements, as these can escalate the horse's anxiety.

How to Calm & Center Yourself

Calming and centering yourself is essential for effective emergency management. Techniques such as deep breathing, grounding exercises, and visualization can help you achieve a state of calm and focus.

- **Breathe Deep**: Inhale deeply through your nose, hold for a few seconds, and then exhale slowly through your mouth. Repeat this several times to *lower your heart rate and reduce anxiety.*

- **Ground & Center**: Stand with your feet firmly planted on the ground, and visualize roots extending from your feet into the earth. This helps you *feel stable and connected.*

- **Visualization**: Picture a calm and successful resolution to the emergency. Visualizing a positive outcome can help you *stay focused and composed.*

Communicating Calmness to Your Horse

Your horse is highly attuned to your emotional state and body language. To communicate calmness, use a soft, steady voice, and gentle touch. Approach your horse slowly and avoid abrupt movements.

For example, if your horse is anxious, placing a reassuring hand on their neck while speaking calmly can help convey your calmness to them. In massage training, this is often referred to as the "mother hand." This is a calm, reassuring touch like your mom may have touched you as a child when you were upset or not feeling well. Your consistent, composed demeanor provides the reassurance they need to settle down.

Congratulations, you're making great strides toward a calm, trust-filled connection with your horse!

Now, let's go even deeper. Your path to a more profound emotional and energetic connection with your horse has just begun—*Visit tab.so/calmhorse or scan the code to continue your journey!*

Chapter 7
Ready for Anything

Assessing and Handling Equine Emergencies

IN ANY STRESSFUL OR emergency, the ability to quickly and accurately assess the scenario is crucial. This involves observing the environment, understanding the nature of the problem, and determining the best course of action. For horse owners and handlers, this means being able to identify signs of distress or injury in your horse and responding in a calm, methodical manner. Your ability to remain composed not only helps you think more clearly but also reassures your horse, preventing their stress levels from escalating.

Observation and Initial Assessment

The first step in any emergency is to observe and assess the situation calmly. Take a moment to breathe deeply and ground yourself, as your horse will look to you for cues on how to react. Quickly survey the environment for any immediate dangers to both you and your horse. For example, if your horse is startled by a loud noise, first ensure that there are no additional hazards like traffic or sharp objects nearby.

Next, evaluate your horse's condition. Look for signs of physical distress or injury, such as limping, swelling, or bleeding. Pay attention to their behavior—are they panicked, lethargic, or displaying unusual behaviors? This initial assessment will guide your next steps and help you determine whether the situation can be managed on your own or if professional help is needed.

Example: Handling an Injury

Imagine you are out on a trail ride and your horse suddenly stumbles, resulting in a visible cut on their leg. Your immediate reaction might be one of panic, but it's essential to maintain your composure to effectively manage the situation.

1. **Calm Yourself First**: Take a few deep breaths to calm your nerves. Remember the emotional regulation techniques discussed in earlier chapters. Your horse will sense your calmness, which can help keep them relaxed.

2. **Assess the Injury**: Approach your horse slowly and observe the wound. Is it bleeding heavily, or is it a minor cut? Check for signs of more severe injury, such as swelling or an inability to bear weight on the affected leg.

3. **Perform Basic First Aid**: If the cut is bleeding heavily, apply pressure with a clean cloth or bandage to control the bleeding. If you have a first aid kit, clean the wound with antiseptic to prevent infection. Your calm and confident handling of the situation will help soothe your horse.

4. **Call the Vet**: For significant injuries, contact your veterinarian immediately.

Explain the situation clearly and follow their instructions. Having your vet's contact information readily available can save valuable time.

5. **Keep Your Horse Calm**: While waiting for the vet, continue to reassure your horse with a calm voice and gentle touch. If possible, move them to a safe, quiet area away from potential stressors.

Responding with Confidence

Responding confidently to emergencies involves practice and preparation. Regularly practicing emergency scenarios can build your confidence and ensure that you and your horse are better prepared when real emergencies occur. This includes rehearsing the steps of basic first aid and knowing how to communicate effectively with your vet.

Practical Steps to Ensure Preparedness

1. **First Aid Training**: Take a course in equine first aid to familiarize yourself with common injuries and appropriate

responses. Knowing how to handle wounds, fractures, and colic can be lifesaving. https://equi-firstaidusa.com/

2. **Emergency Contact List**: Keep a list of emergency contacts, including your veterinarian, an emergency transport service, and nearby equine hospitals. Ensure that this list is easily accessible.

3. **First Aid Kit**: Maintain a well-stocked first aid kit that includes bandages, antiseptics, scissors, and other essential items. Regularly check and replenish supplies as needed.

4. **Regular Drills**: Conduct regular emergency drills to practice staying calm and applying first aid. Include different scenarios to cover a range of potential emergencies.

5. **Know Your Horse**: Understanding your horse's normal behavior and vital signs can help you quickly identify when something is wrong. Regularly check their temperature, pulse, and respiration rates so you have a baseline for comparison.

Assessing and responding to emergencies with a clear mind and steady hand can make a significant difference in the outcome for your horse. By preparing in advance, practicing emergency procedures, and maintaining a calm demeanor, you ensure that you are ready to handle any situation that arises. This preparedness not only enhances your confidence but also strengthens the bond of trust between you and your horse, providing them with the reassurance they need in times of distress.

Healing Together
Post-Emergency Recovery for Horse and Handler

Once an emergency has been managed and immediate threats have been addressed, both the horse and the handler need time to recover. This recovery phase is crucial for physical healing, emotional stabilization, and reinforcing trust. Ensuring that both you and your horse recuperate fully after a stressful situation will help prevent long-term trauma and improve your readiness for future incidents.

Recovery for Your Horse

1. **Physical Healing**: Begin by ensuring that any physical injuries your horse sustained are being properly treated. Follow the veterinarian's advice for wound care, medication, and follow-up visits. Monitor your horse closely for any signs of complications or delayed healing.

2. **Emotional Stabilization**: Horses can experience emotional stress after an emergency. It's important to provide a calm and supportive environment. Spend extra time with your horse, engaging in gentle activities that they enjoy and find soothing. This can include grooming, hand-walking, or simply being present with them in their stable.

3. **Gradual Reintroduction to Routine**: Gradually reintroduce your horse to their normal routine. Start with light activities and slowly increase the intensity as they show signs of comfort and readiness. This gradual process helps to rebuild their confidence and ensures they don't feel

overwhelmed.

4. **Reinforcing Trust**: Use this recovery time to reinforce the bond of trust between you and your horse. Positive reinforcement techniques can be beneficial here. Reward your horse with treats or praise for calm behavior and responsiveness. This reinforces the idea that you are a source of safety and comfort.

Recovery for Yourself

Navigating an emergency can be mentally and physically exhausting for the handler as well. It's essential to acknowledge your own need for recovery and to take proactive steps to manage stress and prevent burnout.

1. **Physical Rest**: Ensure that you get adequate rest after handling an emergency. Physical exertion during a crisis can be taxing, and your body needs time to recover. Take time off from strenuous activities and allow yourself to recuperate.

2. **Emotional Processing**: It's important to

process the emotional impact of the emergency. Talk to a trusted friend, family member, or professional about your experience. Sometimes, simply expressing your thoughts and feelings can help alleviate stress.

3. **Reflection and Learning**: Reflect on the emergency and your response to it. What went well? What could have been handled differently? This reflection is not about self-criticism but about learning and improving your readiness for future situations. Journaling can be a helpful tool for this process.

4. **Utilizing Techniques from the Book**: Revisit the techniques for emotional regulation and mindfulness discussed earlier in the book. Practices such as the Quick Coherence Technique®, deep breathing, mindfulness meditation, and grounding exercises can help stabilize your emotions and restore your sense of calm.

5. **Self-Care Practices**: Engage in activities that promote relaxation and well-being.

This could include yoga, spending time in nature, engaging in a hobby, or simply taking a relaxing bath. Self-care is not a luxury; it's a necessary part of maintaining your health and resilience.

Reinforcing Readiness for the Future

Post-emergency recovery is also a time to reinforce your readiness for future incidents. Consider what you've learned from the experience and how you can apply this knowledge to improve your preparation and response strategies.

1. **Review and Update Emergency Plans**: Review your emergency plans and make any necessary updates based on your recent experience. Ensure that your first aid kit is replenished and that you have a clear plan for different types of emergencies.

2. **Continued Training**: Continue to practice the techniques and drills that help prepare you and your horse for emergencies. Regular training keeps these skills sharp and ensures that both you and your horse

are always ready to respond effectively.

3. **Building a Support Network**: Ensure that you have a reliable support network in place. This can include other horse owners, trainers, and veterinarians. Having a community you can rely on for advice and assistance can make a significant difference in handling emergencies.

Post-emergency recovery is an essential part of the emergency management process. It's a time for healing, reflection, and learning. By taking care of both your horse's needs and your own, you strengthen the bond between you and enhance your readiness for future challenges. Remember to utilize the techniques and strategies discussed throughout this book to support your recovery and continue building a calm, confident relationship with your horse.

Chapter 8
Conclusion

"There is no secret so close as that between a rider and his horse."
Robert Smith Surtees

CONGRATULATIONS, you've made great strides toward a calm, trust-filled connection with your horse!

As we come to the end of this part of your journey, I hope that you feel more equipped to handle stressful situations with your horse and that you understand the profound impact your calmness and presence can have on your equine companion. By integrating the techniques and strategies discussed throughout this book, you can create a safer, more harmonious relationship with your horse, grounded in mutual trust and understanding.

Remember, the key to maintaining calmness lies in consistent practice and self-awareness. Whether you are preparing for potential emergencies, learning to read and respond to your horse's body language, or developing your emotional regulation skills, each step you take will deepen your bond and enhance your ability to navigate challenges with confidence.

Your journey doesn't end here. Continue to practice mindfulness and emotional regulation, both for your benefit and your horse's. Embrace each opportunity to connect with your horse in the present moment, fostering a sense of safety and comfort that will serve you both well in any situation.

Thank you for allowing me to share my experiences and insights with you. Your commitment to improving your relationship with your horse is commendable, and I am confident that the tools you have gained will lead to a more enriching and fulfilling partnership.

CONCLUSION

·♥·♥·♥·♥·♥·

Ready to Take Your Journey Even Further? Your path to a more profound emotional and energetic connection with your horse has just begun—*Visit tab.so/calmhorse or scan the code to continue your journey!*

Wishing you many calm & confident rides ahead!

Bettyann

·♥·♥·♥·♥·♥·

Pay It Forward!

Now that you have everything you need to create a calm, confident connection with your horse, it's time to pass on your newfound knowledge and show other readers where they can find the same help.

If you enjoyed "Calm Human, Calm Horse" and found it helpful, please consider leaving a review on Amazon. Your review will help other horse enthusiasts discover this valuable resource and pass your passion for harmonious horse-human relationships forward.

Thank you for your help. The journey to calm, confident horsemanship is kept alive when we pass on our knowledge – and you're helping me to do just that.

Simply scan the QR code below or go to https://tab.so/reviewchch to leave your review on Amazon.

Thank you from the bottom of my heart.

Bettyann Cernese

References

Childre, D. & Martin, H. (1999). *The HeartMath Solution: The Institute of HeartMath's Revolutionary Program for Engaging the Power of the Heart's Intelligence.* HarperOne.

Hallberg, L. (2008). *Walking the Way of the Horse: Exploring the Power of the Horse-Human Relationship.* iUniverse.

HeartMath Institute. (n.d.). Quick Coherence® Technique for Adults. Retrieved from .

McGreevy, P. (2004). *Equine Behavior: A Guide for Veterinarians and Equine Scientists.* Saunders.

Miller, R. (2007). *Understanding the Ancient Secrets of the Horse's Mind.* Eclipse Press.

Siegel, D. J. (2010). *The Mindful Therapist: A Clinician's Guide to Mindsight and Neural Integration.* W. W. Norton & Company.

Waring, G. H. (2003). *Horse Behavior.* Noyes Publications.

Warren-Smith, A. K., & McGreevy, P. D. (2008). *The use of blended positive and negative reinforcement in shaping the halt response of horses (Equus caballus).* Animal Welfare, 17(2), 231-238.

About the Author

Passionate about horsemanship and the transformative power it holds, Bettyann Cernese is a BodyMind Horsemanship Guide with over 30 years of experience working with  horses and their human companions. She combines her expertise as a massage therapist, energy healer, and equine guided life coach to help horsewomen unlock their true potential and deepen their connection with their horses.

Bettyann's journey began with a spirited horse named J.J., whose unpredictability and spookiness led her to discover the profound impact of emotional regulation on horsemanship. By managing her own energy and emotions, Bettyann transformed her relationship with J.J., leading to a harmonious partnership both in dressage competitions and on tranquil trail rides.

With a commitment to conscious horsemanship, Bettyann's approach is rooted in the PEACE Framework – presence, empathy, awareness, connection, and emotion regulation. Her holistic methods are designed to enhance horsemanship skills and enrich overall well-being, fostering a meaningful and fulfilling connection between horse and rider.

When she's not guiding fellow horsewomen, Bettyann enjoys camping and trail riding with her husband and their Missouri Fox Trotters. Join her on this incredible journey and discover the transformative power of calmness and connection in horsemanship.

Made in the USA
Middletown, DE
30 October 2024